Meditation for Beginners

How to Easily Meditate and Relieve Stress for a Happy, Healthy and Peaceful Life

Brian Covey

book.

Table of Contents

Introduction

Before we begin, I would like to thank you for downloading this book, "Meditation for Beginners: How to Easily Meditate and Relieve Stress for a Happy, Healthy and Peaceful Life." I hope you enjoy reading it.

Have you ever practiced meditation before? You might have had some experience with meditation in the past, or you might be completely new to meditating. In either case, this book is the perfect guide to help you learn about meditation and use it to improve your life in different ways. Meditation is definitely one of the best ways to lead a happier, stress-free, and peaceful existence. Who wouldn't want to lead a peaceful life? I am sure everyone does, and meditation is the key to unlocking the door to tranquility.

There are no restrictions, and anyone can practice meditation. It has been practiced in various cultures for centuries and will surely continue to be practiced for many more to come. If you want to learn about everything, from the basics of meditation to different techniques, this is the perfect book for you.

This book will guide you through simple meditation practices that will help improve your focus, deal with stress, and lead a healthier and happier life in general. It is important for everyone to learn to let go of certain things and shift their attention to those things that truly matter. Meditation is a tool that can help you do this.

So, if you are ready to learn more, then let's begin.

Chapter One: An Introduction to Meditation

For a long time, meditation was associated with mysticism, and people considered it best left to yogis or other spiritual gurus. However, times have changed, and people have started to open themselves up to the myriad benefits of meditation. People no longer assume that meditation is something that Buddhist monks practice as a part of their religious routine. Meditation is a great practice for one and all. Meditation not only helps you spiritually, but it also helps improve your physical and mental health over time.

What is Meditation?

Meditation is a unique and holistic approach to training your mind to be calmer and more positive while pushing away any negativity. It is not just about sitting cross-legged, closing your eyes and chanting "ohm." There are different ways to meditate. The physical silence that you are asked to observe while meditating also applies to your surroundings.

Meditation should help you empty all thoughts from your mind. One of the essential things you will learn while meditating is that you must maintain good posture, remain quiet, and focus on your breathing. You will learn to empty out all your thoughts and feelings, and you will learn how to be more present and focus on the here and now. Your body will be more relaxed, and you will be able to concentrate on every breath you inhale and exhale.

This simple act of meditation will help you escape from all the anxiety or stress that might bother you in your day-to-day life.

You don't have to focus on your past or worry about your future at this time. The past is gone, and the future is yet to come. The one aspect that you have control over is your present; however, most people find it extremely difficult to keep their focus on the present.

Meditation will help change this. Initially, it might be difficult to fight the natural tendency of your mind to wander off. Slowly but surely, you will learn to train your mind to concentrate on what is important.

The art of meditation has been practiced for thousands of years and its benefits are well documented. It has survived for centuries and still thrives in various cultures around the world. Although it is traditionally considered more of an eastern practice, the western world has embraced meditation over the last decade. This is because of all the different benefits associated with meditation. It can be an enlightening experience to keep an open mind instead of being filled with doubts. You need to trust in the positive effects of meditation if you want it to be effective.

Meditation is a practice that everyone could benefit from learning. The modern-day lifestyle can be stressful at times and can be too hectic to handle. Our lives, in general, have become stressful and tiring. No one seems to be truly happy and satisfied with the life they lead, regardless of whether they are rich and successful or not.

Meditating every day can help anyone find the strength to get through each day in a positive way. Meditation will help you deal with troubling and complicated thoughts or feelings that might have been bothering you until now. Meditation will allow you to get over the weariness of daily life. Every time you meditate, you will be able to see a positive change in yourself and will feel better too.

Meditation is one of the best practices that a person can include in their daily routine. Making meditation a habit will benefit you in so many ways as you will learn in this book. It is an effortless practice and offers numerous benefits. There are several ways in which you can practice meditation. The effects of meditation also differ from one person to another. At times, the techniques that might have worked for others might not necessarily work for you, but after reading this book, you will have a variety of options to choose from so you can find the technique that is right for you.

History of Meditation

Those who practice meditation swear by its ability to bring positive change into their lives, but where does meditation originate from and what is its history?

The precise history of meditation is still uncertain. The earliest records of the practice of meditation dates back to roughly 1500 years B.C. It appeared to have been an essential element of the earlier people of the Vedic, or early Hindu civilization and was professed by different schools of thought in India. During the periods between the 6th to 4th B.C, the Chinese Taoist and Indian Buddhist customs started to develop their own renditions of the practice of meditation. Further west, early types of meditation practice were introduced by remarkable figures such as Philo of Alexandria, the Desert Fathers of the Middle East, and Saint Augustine.

The Beginning of Meditation

The English word "meditation" originates from *meditatum*, a

Latin expression meaning "to think." Although it cannot be accurately pinpointed when this practice came about, researchers and experts believe that the practice of meditation[1] probably started before the earliest available records and before the introduction of present-day form of the practice. For the researchers to determine the origins of meditation, they would essentially need to translate old transcripts and decipher pictographs to scour for any references to this practice.

A few archeological discoveries showed that the early shamans were practitioners of some form of meditation. Their insight was passed on from one generation to the next, and this established the framework for present-day meditation.

It is difficult to pinpoint the origins of meditation since there are a lot of different practices that fall under the "meditation" umbrella. Does it refer to a form of mindfulness? Is it contemplation and introspection? Or does it refer to a practice of chanting to induce oneself into a trance-like state?

---

[1] "Where Does Meditation Come From? Meditation History & Origins". (2019). Retrieved from https://mindworks.org/blog/history-origins-of-meditation/

Chapter Two: Benefits of Meditation

Meditation has numerous benefits for your body, mind, and soul. In this section, you will learn why you should start practicing meditation. If you had any doubts or reservations about the effectiveness of meditation, then by the end of this chapter, your perspective toward meditation will be changed.

Meditation Helps to Reduce Stress

The modern-day lifestyle that we lead is hectic and inadvertently leads to stress and anxiety on some level. Stress has become one of the most common problems that people suffer from these days. You may think that you can put it off or might have resigned yourself to the fact that it is a part of your life. However, stress can lead to a myriad of health problems like high blood pressure, an increase in the risk of cardiovascular disorders, and insomnia, just to name a few. The stress chemical in the body is called cortisol. Your body can usually regulate the levels of cortisol within it, but the more your stress levels, the higher the amount of cortisol secreted. This can cause issues like panic attacks. Cortisol secretion needs to be regulated. All of these issues can, however, be dealt with using the help of meditation. It will help in reducing your stress levels and help you deal with anxiety-inducing issues in a productive manner. Overall, by practicing meditation, you will notice a decline in your stress and anxiety levels.

Meditation Helps Keep Emotions Under Control

Humans are emotional creatures. However, it can be hard for us to control our emotions at times, and this can have dangerous consequences. This is especially true in the present world that we live in. The increased amount of pressure and anxiety you experience can cause a build-up of many negative feelings. If you let emotions like anger build up, it will only harm you. Not just you, but also those around you. Meditation will help you maintain your calm and stay composed even in the face of adversity. When you are able to stay calm, then it is easier to rationalize your thoughts. Apart from this, it will also help you make better decisions. You must not let your emotions control you, and meditation will help you get a handle on your emotions.

Meditation Increases Serotonin Secretion

You might have heard of serotonin, the "happy hormone." The human body secretes various hormones that have a huge impact on how you think and feel. These chemicals in your body will affect how happy, sad, or angry you are. Serotonin is a chemical that helps people stay happy. Studies show that regular meditation helps in increasing serotonin secretion. This chemical has a positive effect on your mind and body. Low levels of serotonin are observed in people suffering from depression and other mental health issues. So, meditation is one of the most effective means of tackling depression.

Meditation Improves the Ability to Focus

Having the ability to focus better is something everyone aims for in life. However, most people have trouble with this. Being able to focus can help you in so many ways. If you are a student, it will help you study better. If you just have certain goals in life, you will be able to focus on those goals and work accordingly. Lack of focus can make you lose track of what you do and lead an undisciplined life. Research shows that those who practice meditation tend to have a better ability to focus on their tasks and perform better than those who don't practice meditation. Different meditation techniques will help you hone your ability to focus and enhance your cognitive abilities.

Meditation Increases Creativity

It is also said that meditation can get your creative juices flowing. When you meditate and reduce your stress levels, your brain is allowed to function better, and you can be more creative. This creative ability is often negatively impacted by high stress levels. Meditation will help you embrace the good and the bad in your life without harming your happiness or health.

Meditation Increases Empathy and the Ability to Connect

It is important for you to learn how to empathize and connect with others if you want better relationships. Meditation will help you learn compassion and thus act compassionately towards people. People who meditate tend to have an increased capacity for kindness and understanding towards others. You will be able to think of things from others' perspectives and react to situations in a better way. Meditation can enhance this empathetic ability and improve your social interactions.

Meditation Helps Improve Relationships

Do you feel like your relationships with your loved ones could use some extra help? Meditation can help you with this. As mentioned, meditation helps increase your empathy, and this will help you immensely. It helps to increase your awareness so that you can pick up on cues from those around you. This will help you understand how they are feeling in certain situations. By getting a read on the situation, it will be easier for you to react and respond in the right way. Apart from this, it also helps reduce any chances of misunderstandings cropping up. Once your emotions are stabilized, the chances of letting any negativity through will decrease.

Meditation Enhances Memory

Do you feel like you have become forgetful? There could be many reasons behind this, stress being the main culprit. Regardless of what the cause is, meditation can help improve your memory, if practiced regularly. You will be able to focus on things and become more conscious of your surroundings and your own self. You will also be able to retain information for longer and thus be less forgetful. Meditation can be a great memory-enhancing tool regardless of what you do or what your age is.

Meditation Improves Immunity

Another benefit of meditation is that it is a holistic way of boosting your body's immune system. If you feel like you get sick too often or just want to be healthier, you should try meditation. Various meditation techniques like yoga are known to help in strengthening the immune system. By meditating regularly, you will notice a positive change in your overall immunity.

Meditation Helps You Overcome Addictions

Addictions are a serious affliction that can be really hard to contend with. It requires a lot of self-control and discipline to let go of any type of addiction. This could be smoking, alcoholism, or just about any unhealthy addiction that has a negative impact on your health and well-being. It's not just the addictions that affect your physical health. There are other addictions like watching too much pornography, using excessive social media, binge eating, etc. These affect your body and mind in many negative ways. There are certain meditation techniques, like Vipassana meditation, which is often used to help addicts overcome powerful addictions. Just meditating will not solve all your problems, but it is a great tool to help you move forward and leave your addictions behind. So, if you or anyone you know suffers from an addiction, trying meditation is a good place to start.

Meditation Benefits Cardiovascular Health

It is actually common sense that meditation is good for the heart. In the event that you observe how regular meditation helps you when you need to relax and how it decreases your tendency to be anxious, at that point is there any good reason why it shouldn't also help reduce the risk of cardiovascular issues, similar to hypertension?

For a considerable length of time, many assumed that to be the case, yet a couple of specialists appeared to be intrigued enough to research and document the physical outcomes on the heart after meditating. The leading researcher to explore this connection was Herbert Benson from Harvard. His important book, distributed in the mid-1970s, *The Relaxation Response,* raised a lot of discussions inside intellectual circles. Through medical testing, he showed that changes occurred in the body.

At first, other colleagues were skeptical of his discoveries. Nobody had ever genuinely thought that there could be medical advantages related to this meditative training. In any case, his testing withstood the thorough investigation conducted by others. In the last two decades, mainstream researchers picked up progressively genuine enthusiasm for the subject. The research started, yet more explicitly, the *American Heart Association Journal* published an article that reported the ability of meditation to bring down an individual's risk factors that are associated with all types of cardiovascular illness.

The *American Journal of Hypertension*[2] recently also published positive reviews on the medical advantages of meditation. In this research, it was found that a gathering of meditating people viably brought down their blood pressure, contrasted with a second group that didn't meditate. The decrease in blood pressure for these individuals was so apparent, truth be told, that the meditators had the option to reduce their utilization of antihypertensive drugs by about 25 percent. Stress is related to something beyond coronary illness.

Stress can cause disruption in a lot of physiological functions. At the end of the day, when you're worried all the time, it manifests in the form of any number of medical issues. One of the systems you may have noticed this in is through gastrointestinal dysfunctions. It's not "all in your head," it's been extensively recorded that changes in physiology and hormones happen in your body in relation to stress. These cause various stomach issues, as a response to a distressing

---

[2] Yang, H., Wu, X., & Wang, M. (2017). The Effect of Three Different Meditation Exercises on Hypertension: A Network Meta-Analysis. *Evidence-based complementary and alternative medicine : eCAM, 2017,* 9784271. doi:10.1155/2017/9784271

condition - either acute or chronic.

A few people also experience sleep disorders due to stress. In some of these cases, the sleep issues are linked with irritable bowel syndrome. Fortunately, these physical changes can be reduced and eased through consistent meditation practice.

Meditation Aids Weight Loss

It's hard to be your best when you're troubled with weight issues. Sadly, numerous people who are overweight do not have a good self-image and lack a sense of self-worth. Without that, they may believe that their ideal life is far out of their grasp. Meditation can do something amazing here, in two different ways. To begin with, it's not unusual to start eating when you're stressed out.

If you are someone who does this, you realize that what you go after first is generally something salty, sugary or greasy. It's not about your absence of self-restraint - blame the hormonal changes related with too much stress instead. Your body craves this kind of unhealthy food when it is under distress.

A lot of research demonstrates that the physical impact of stress on your body can be greatly diminished through meditation. It starts by diminishing the body's cortisol level, which can then mitigate those obstinate yearnings for food. Maybe meditating doesn't offer that equivalent comfort that you get from the bag of chips, candy, or fries (or even all three). Yet, it can help curb those cravings in any case. This is a part of the process that will allow people to pick up a superior mental self-image, which, then, empowers them to concentrate on seeking the life that they need to lead. Stress is very slippery. It penetrates your entire being. Maybe, however, its most notable impeding impacts are on the person's immunity. Consider it. How often have you caught a cold or even the flu following an unpleasant event?

Meditation can definitely help you with this also. People under pressure are known to have decreased amounts of basic white blood cells, which are essential for battling foreign attacking microscopic organisms and infections, which can cause cold, influenza, and other illnesses. Meditation is undoubtedly now seen as a great way to insightfully deal with the stress in your life.

Meditation Helps Manage Headaches

A headache is one of the most common signs that your body is experiencing too much stress. What's more, it's difficult to concentrate on what is important to you when a headache is floating over the majority of your thoughts. It's hard to think, and at the same time, it's hard to use sound judgment, and it's tough to enjoy yourself. Maybe it doesn't come as anything unexpected that meditation is the ideal method to loosen up those muscles and suppress that pain.

In addition to the fact that it works for most people, its positive effects are likewise scientifically confirmed. Even for a brief timeframe, going within yourself as meditation allows you to do changes in your brain waves to another higher state. This is a dimension of awareness that is known to help advance the process of healing. The takeaway here is that through meditation, you can adjust your brain waves. Researchers were once convinced that an individual's brain waves are unchangeable. They trusted that we are brought into the world with specific patterns, and these couldn't be modified, despite our ability to switch between different dimensions of cognizance.

Today, however, it's broadly acknowledged that your brain waves *can* be changed—and meditation is one way in which this can be accomplished. The most recent studies have taken a look at people who have been meditating for over fifteen years. Long-term meditation changes the functioning of the brain, which permits the individuals who meditate to achieve a more elevated amount of mindfulness than the individuals who don't. In any case, nothing is preventing you right now from disposing of that migraine through a ten-or fifteen-minute session of meditation, so why not try it?

As you can see, meditation has a lot of benefits for those who practice it regularly. There are actually more ways in which it helps than just the ones mentioned above. If you genuinely want to experience the benefits of meditation, you need to get started. The next few chapters will help you learn more about meditation and help you begin your own meditative practice.

Chapter Three: The Process of Meditation

In this section, you will learn more about the process of meditation and what it entails.

The Right Posture

Start with the right posture. You can either be seated on a mat or a cushion. Elderly people or people with backaches can be seated on a chair, with their backs erect. It is not necessary to be seated in an asana position while meditating. Just ensure that you keep your backs straight as slumping can distract your mind. Relax your body and imagine that you're floating up in the sky.

The Myth

It is a widespread belief that one has to keep his or her eyes closed during meditation, but the fact is that keeping your eyes closed during meditation can cause your mind to drift. Meditating with your eyes open can keep your mind alert and present. Keep your gaze soft and stay focused while you meditate. See what works better for you. It is absolutely necessary to be comfortable when you meditate. Some people prefer keeping their eyes shut as that works best for them. If you are one of these people, then feel free to carry on in the way you're most comfortable with.

Focus

This part takes lots of patience and practice. Our mind is always wandering, and it takes effort to focus. Sometimes when we are driving, our mind is preoccupied with thoughts that we won't realize the memory of our drive until we have reached our destination, as if were on "autopilot." Or even while traveling on a train or bus as you are staring out the window distracted with thoughts, you won't realize how an hour or more just passed by. Once you start meditating, you will be able to focus well. When we think of focus, we usually think "intense concentration," but that's not the case, and does not work while you are meditating. When you meditate, you have to have a softer direction that is directed towards your awareness. The key is to have a relaxed state of mind, even If your mind keeps wandering. Stay calm and focus on your breaths.

Breathing

Being aware and paying attention to your breathing pattern is the easiest way to get into the state of awareness while meditating. This also gets you to actually "be" in the present moment. You can meditate anywhere through this technique: in a crowded bus or your workspace. Simply pay attention as you breathe in and out of your nostrils. Remain as calm and relaxed as you can while you do this. Start counting as you breathe until you reach the number 5 and gradually increase the number.

Counting Breaths

This is one way to be aware of your breaths, and it works.

Count as you let your breaths out "one breath," "two breaths," "three breaths," and so on. You can go on for as many breaths as you want and some days when you don't seem to be in the mood you can do at least five counts. You will see how that will make you feel better and lighter. If you find yourself getting lost in between counts, simply restart and repeat the breath counts all over again.

Thoughts

Many people misunderstand meditation to be a process where one needs to put a halt to their thoughts. But that's not true. Meditation simply requires you to be aware and observe your thoughts. When you try to force your thoughts to stop they will come back to you as negative emotions, so it is better you don't avoid your thoughts. Instead, embrace your scattered thoughts and make peace with them. You will see them fading away. Once you have achieved that, get back to focusing on your breathing.

Emotions

Emotions can be a big distraction when you meditate. Our minds can overthink and create various feelings. Emotions like shame and anger will not allow you to move on from the past. Emotions like fear keep us away from the future and positive changes. The only way to beat emotions is the same way we ought to beat negative thoughts. Embrace your feelings, and you will see yourself letting go of all the emotions that have been impacting you, and you can then get back with the breathing exercises and meditation.

Silence

You will find tons of meditation audios on YouTube and other meditational sites, but none of those will ever compare to the beauty of silence. Meditating in silence can be a blissful experience. Music can sometimes drown all the voices in your head, but only so they could come later on as more significant negative thoughts. Meditating in silence allows your mind to be free, and you will feel peaceful. There is a sense of tranquility in being able to sit in silence. With practice, your inner silence meets the outer silence while allowing you to rest in the moment completely. You will be calmer, and you will experience clarity in thought.

Length

You don't have to sit hours meditating. You can start by meditating for 10 minutes at first and then gradually increase the length of time. The duration does not matter; consistency does. Do not be disheartened if you are unable to meditate for more than 10 minutes because that is still an achievement. There are people who do it for an hour, and there are others who meditate for 10 minutes. Do what you can, and when you reach the 25-minute mark, you will notice quicker changes. Don't be demotivated just because you can't reach a certain number of minutes. Do it correctly and be consistent. That's what really adds to your meditation success.

Place

You can meditate anywhere you feel comfortable. There are no rules, and it's about your comfort place. Not *too* comfortable, like your bed, but somewhere you feel relaxed and at ease. Typically while thinking of someone meditating, we think of someone seated with their eyes closed in the middle of the forest, but that is not absolutely necessary. Amidst nature is a peaceful and ideal place to meditate but you can have that same sense of peace inside your house too. You can make a shrine or a meditation room or simply make your sitting area a bit special, so you feel at peace and ease whenever you sit down at a particular place to meditate. You can work with anything that works well for you. If you want a nice candle-lit room, go for it. If you want to meditate out in nature, then go out in your backyard or a garden and relax. As long as you are comfortable with the place you choose, no place is ever a wrong place to meditate.

Enjoyment

You may have heard some people calling meditation fun, something they enjoy, and even something they find addictive. You must wonder why. Well, enjoyment doesn't necessarily mean having feelings of excitement and glee. Enjoyment can also mean a feeling of satisfaction, bliss, a sense of well-being and a peaceful experience in which you are just genuinely happy. Once you start meditating, you will experience it all. There are people who claim that meditation gets them high. The feeling of ecstasy can be unleashed through meditation. This happens once we let go of all the negative thoughts and emotions that were holding us back from experiencing this powerful sensation. You will start getting addicted to the feeling that meditation leaves you with. You will notice how each time it leaves you happier and lighter.

There are three underlying principles of meditation:

1. Focus and concentration is a must. Being aware of the present is the number one principle.

2. Bring back those wandering thoughts, be as gentle as possible, and restart if you find your mind wandering.

3. Ignore irrelevant thoughts, distractions, and bodily sensations that hamper your meditation process.

While the basis of all meditation is the same, there are a lot of options for you to choose when it comes to deciding how to stop your mind from getting distracted.

This book introduces you to these with a tried and practical approach.

Movement Meditation

This is for some of us who tend to get restless while meditating. This meditation, as the name suggests, is for people with hectic schedules. The thing about this is, it allows you to accomplish more even though you are slowing down. It is not always practical to be in a rush and trying to multitask. You need to take things slow at times and just focus on getting them done right.

This meditation works it two ways: it helps you slow down a little, and also keeps your focal point so you are aware and present in your day. This method centers and focuses on your physical and mental state.

You start this meditation by focusing on the larger movements of your body, like your legs and arms, then you slowly move your focus towards the small movements of your body, doing this for one minute will also help. While doing this, focus mentally on the extensive body movements as well as the small ones. This is also an excellent method to prepare you to focus attention on your breaths.

You can easily adapt this practice, don't limit this to just preparing for your meditation. All you need to do is slow down on your performance. This forces you to pay full attention to your breathing pattern. You can even do this while carrying out menial chores like doing the dishes. The key to it is that you have to be sure of being completely present. It will allow you to notice small details that you would otherwise have ignored.

Conceptual Meditation

Conceptual meditation is another great tool. You need to select something as a focal point. This could be a simple object, or you could be thinking of a particular issue that is bothering you. Your focal point could also be something broader, like love.

While meditating the focal point, you have to start examining your thoughts, and you need to focus on all the different aspects involved. You should try to avoid judging these thoughts as they come up in your mind. All you need to do is increase your awareness of them and keep moving on to any thoughts that arise. You don't have to stop and judge what is bad and what is good.

The goal of this meditation is to find the "untruth" in that topic. It will help you to see things from a different perspective and allow you to change your views on certain things. A few sessions of this type of meditation will allow you to do this effectively. You will be able to find solutions to issues that previously seemed too difficult to manage. It will also help you identify new goals in your life.

Walking Meditation

We all know that walking is one of the simplest yet most effective ways to maintain good physical health. A nice long walk can also help you clear your mind and shake off some stress. However, have you ever considered it as a meditative tool? Although you might be skeptical of this, if it is done the right way, walking meditation can be quite helpful. You just have to shift your attention.

Walking meditation will allow you to observe thoughts and feelings that you might normally not pay attention to. While practicing walking meditation, you will be able to discover things that some others already know, but you did not. Taking a walk is helpful in so many ways. It allows you to clearly think of certain concerns and release the worry. You are able to experience the whole moment and be more present.

Chapter Four: How to Meditate Effectively

Now that you want to begin practicing meditation, you have to consider how to do it as effectively as possible. This section will help you learn how you can practice meditation in an effective way.

Begin Slowly

Keep in mind to not get sucked into some of the meditation strategies that are out there. Some of them will require you to sit for long hours on end, while others may have a series of directions on how you carry out breathing amid meditation, on how you sit in a particular position and a big heap of stuff that is, at its core, insignificant. When you are an apprentice at meditation, you should try to begin this practice slowly. Rather than instantly hopping into longer meditations, begin with sitting alone without anyone to disturb you for around 5 minutes every day. Following a few weeks of doing this, try to stretch the time out to 10 minutes. Keep adding to your meditation time when you think you can. Try not to push yourself too much because the length of the time doesn't make a difference. It's how consistently committed you are to this training. This is the thing that truly matters.

It's Simple

In the event that it feels too difficult, you are probably not doing it right. You may be trying to force yourself to stop all your thoughts or being too hard on yourself. Try not to give yourself a chance to become too obsessed with the subtleties of the meditation technique. There is no ideal space, time, or ideal perspective that you have to adhere to in order to meditate properly. These things are just minor details that don't matter in the big picture. When you meditate, it should feel simple and normal, regardless of whether it means sitting quietly while you are using your computer, or just driving in your vehicle.

Adhere to a Particular Method

Don't fixate on using the correct meditation method and keep shifting things around, trying new techniques each and every day. Maybe just pick one technique you can identify with and stick to it regardless of anything else. Pursue that technique persistently for a month if you want it to begin working for you.

Be Kind to Yourself First

This ought to be your mantra for all your life. It's one of the most important rules to remember when you are doing anything, including meditation. Meditation is for you to realign your vitality and enable the energy to flow effectively through your mind and body. You have to make peace with where you are as opposed to constantly beating yourself up about where you should have been. The same applies to your meditation practice. In the event that you avoid your meditation session for a day or two, be forgiving to yourself and have the persistence to proceed with the meditation the next day. Missing a day of meditation is not something to worry too much about, just don't make it a habit.

Practice Patience

For our entire lives, we put so much pressure on ourselves to be the ideal version of ourselves, only to later realize that flawlessness is essentially a myth. Meditation is intended to get rid of such pressure from our lives. In the event that you are on a journey to achieve perfection even while meditating, I ask you this: What's the point? The point of consistently meditating is to give yourself a break while trying to achieve a sense of harmony between your brain and body. Practice self-compassion without constraining yourself to meditate at a specific time or spot. Just be patient with yourself.

Don't be Judgmental

Try not to pass judgment on anybody in your life and above all else, don't pass judgment on yourself. Nothing is set in stone. Everybody has the free will to live their lives in the manner in which they choose to, and there's no compelling reason to characterize something as bad and good or wrong and right. When you let go of such judgment, you will find that it is easy to meditate. Meditation is tied in with removing your protective barrier from all the negative events throughout your life, so you can have a better experience later on. In order to do that, you should be in a space where you are totally non-judgmental about everything in your daily life.

Set a Morning Schedule

Once again I repeat: don't be excessively hard on yourself while you do this. While meditation can be performed at pretty much any time, a morning schedule will surely be progressively effective to guarantee that your day goes well. Making it a point to meditate for a couple of minutes each and every morning will allow you to have superior control on your feelings and basic capacity to make decisions for the rest of the day. Additionally, it's simpler to persuade yourself to stick to something amid the beginning of the day than it is at the end of a monotonous day.

Utilize Guided Meditations

Guided meditations work very well for those who have just begun meditation. As a first timer, when you first begin meditation, you may find meditation techniques a little difficult. Guided meditations are fundamentally just soundtracks intended to guide you through each phase of meditation. It's valuable for people who need assistance during their meditation sessions. The best part about these audio files is that for the most part, they are totally free and you can easily find a lot of them on the Internet. With the assistance of guided meditation, you won't need to stress over what to do right away. You can just unwind while adhering to the directions being given to you via these audio files.

Get a Meditation Buddy

Doesn't everything get simpler when having a companion with you? You can get yourself a meditation partner and share the experience together. Being accountable to someone for your meditation practice is a great way to remain persistent. Following each other's advancement, sharing positive thoughts or helping each other remain centered can go far in guaranteeing that you practice meditation as a lifestyle. As people, we are bound to stick to something when we have made a promise to somebody that we will do so.

Find a Meditation Support Group

Can't find a mate to meditate with? Join a support group. These gatherings include a lot of individuals who have dedicated themselves to meditation. Here, you won't just discover individuals who can spur you on, but you will also have a huge gathering of individuals supporting you at whatever point you may stumble off track. Making meditation a habit may not come easy to many of us, and mindfulness groups can allow us to accomplish our meditative goals.

Chapter Five: Meditation Techniques and Routines

In this section, you will learn about some of the various meditation techniques that are practiced by people around the world. You can try any of these when you delve into meditating yourself.

Buddhist Meditation Techniques

Vipassana Meditation

Vipassana meditation is an ancient traditional Buddhist practice that dates back to the 6th century B.C. "Vipassana" is derived from a Pali word meaning "clear sight" or "insight." This meditation is practiced to gain clarity in our mind and teaches us about the mindfulness of breathing, it was popularized by the Vipassana movement and S.N. Goenka, and is popularly known as "mindfulness" in the west. The first stage in this meditation is to stabilize the mind, so it starts with the mindfulness of breath to gain concentration. This meditation requires focused attention. Then the practice moves to the next stage of developing "clear insight." This includes observing the bodily sensations and the mental phenomena moment by moment, but not sticking to any of the sensations.

Ideally, one should be seated on the floor on a cushion, crossed legged with an erect spine.

Close your eyes and try to develop concentration by being aware of your breaths. Focus your attention on your breath, be aware of the movements in your abdomen area as it rises and falls back. You can also focus your attention on your breaths thrown out of the nostrils and touching your upper lip, although this is more advanced and requires practice. Focusing on your breath allows you to notice other bodily sensations like the sounds, feelings, and emotions. Pay attention and be aware of these phenomena as they emerge and then return your focus on the sensation of breathing while keeping the other thoughts and sensation as "background music."

Zazen Meditation

"Zazen" meditation means "seated meditation" in Japanese. It was practiced by an Indian monk named Bodhi Dharma in the 6th century. This meditation also has roots that are from the Chinese Zen Buddhism tradition (Ch'an). In the west, it was popularized by Dogen Zenji around 1200 to 1253 B.C., the founder of the Soto Zen movement. Zazen meditation is the primary practice of the Zen Buddhist tradition. The meaning of this particular style of meditation varies, but in general, it means "insight" and "nature of existence." It is practiced while being seated on a floor over a mat or a cushion with crossed legs; you can even be seated on a chair with your spine erect. Focus on your breath and the movement of the breath as it goes in and out your nose. Count each breath in your mind to keep your mind focused on the breaths. Start with 10 and move backward until you arrive at 1 and then start all over from 10 again. In case you lose attention, then resume from number 10 all over again. There is another way of practicing this meditation known as Shikantaza, which means, "just sitting." This involves simply remaining seated and being present at the moment, observing and staying aware of what passes through your mind and around you.

Mindfulness Meditation

This form of mediation is an adaptation of Buddhist meditation practices like Vipassana meditation and Vietnamese Zen Buddhism practices. Mindfulness is the direct translation of the Buddhist term "Sati Anapanasati."

John Kabat Zinn was one of the main influencers of mindfulness who made this term and practice popular in the west. His techniques are used in several health clinics and hospitals to this day.

This kind of meditation is the practice of focusing on the present moment, like the meditation techniques mentioned above, paying attention to the body and its sensations and emotions without being judgmental about it. This meditation requires a person to be seated on a cushion on the floor with a straight unsupported back. Pay close attention to your breaths. Be aware of what is going on in and around you. When your mind gets distracted with sounds, thoughts, and sensations, recognize that you have been distracted and bring your attention back around to being aware of your breathing and your presence. You can perform this technique while performing other activities like eating, walking, talking, doing chores, etc. The technique is to be *aware* of what is happening but not *living* in it, not dwelling on it. It is important that you learn to enjoy this practice while you do your daily deeds. When you are speaking, be aware and pay attention to the words you speak and how you speak. If you are walking, be aware of your body and its movements, the sounds you hear as you walk and the sensations you feel when you walk. Listen and pay attention to the sounds you hear while performing these techniques, whether you are seated or in movement while doing this meditation. This technique also happens to be one of the best types of meditation for beginners.

Metta Meditation

Metta comes from a Pali word, which means "kindness, goodwill, and benevolence." This technique also comes from Buddhist traditions, specifically from the Tibetan and Theravada lineages. The benefits of performing this technique include the development of compassion, positive emotions, boosting your ability to empathize, having a loving attitude towards oneself and others, having increased self-acceptance, as well as the feeling of having a greater purpose in one's life.

While performing this meditation technique, the performer should be seated in a meditation position with closed eyes and is required to generate feelings of kindness and love towards yourself and other beings. It is suggested that you think of yourself with love at the initial stage and then go forward with the same feelings while thinking of a good friend and then to focus on a person you have a neutral feeling for, then finally a difficult person, think of all four persons: yourself, your favorite person, the person you have neutral feelings for and the person you have not liked for some reason, in an equally loving and compassionate way. And then move on to feeling kindness, compassion, and love for the entire universe.

Develop a feeling of happiness, positivity, and well-being towards all creatures and human life around you. This practice can be helped by using affirmations that help you evoke warm-hearted feelings by visualizing other people's suffering and sending them love, peace, and happiness. The more you practice this meditation, the more joyous and peaceful you will feel. It is especially useful for people who are hard on themselves and others or people who want to improve their relationships. It is for people who are selfless and selfish. These meditation techniques help your general level of happiness and make you a peace-loving person. It is also recommended by Buddhist teachers as an antidote when one suffers from insomnia, anger issues, or nightmares.

Hindu Meditation Techniques

Mantra Meditation

Also known as OM Meditation, a mantra is a word without any particular meaning. Mantras are repetitive words that are like a tool for the mind to focus. It is not an affirmation that is used to convince oneself. Mantras are generally related to the vibration that is associated with the sound. Mantras are used not only in Hindi traditions but also Buddhism, Sikhism, Jainism, and Daoism. Just like any other meditation style, this technique is performed while being seated cross-legged and with the spine erect. The performer then starts to chant mantras repeatedly in his mind or silently over and over again. It is also necessary for the practitioner becomes aware of one's breathing while chanting the mantras. As you chant these mantras repetitively, it creates a vibration that is meant to allow the mind to experience deeper levels of alertness. Repetition of mantras helps the mind disconnect from unnecessary thoughts that clutter your mind. Mantra is also viewed as an ancient word that is powerful and has lots of subtle intentions that, when used correctly, can help us connect to the spiritual world for a deeper understanding of both oneself and the universe. Traditional people practice repetition of mantras for 108 or 1008 times, and beads are used to keep count of the words as you meditate through chanting your mantras. It is said that people find it easier to meditate chanting mantras than just focusing on one's breaths. It is easy, especially because there are fewer chances of the mind to keep racing through illogical thoughts as you are using words that help keep you focused on the present, and this demands constant attention.

Transcendental Meditation

This meditation was introduced by a yogi named Maharishi Mahesh in 1955 in India. In the late 1960s the Beatles and other noted celebrities found an interest in this yogi and his meditation techniques, and it gave Maharishi Mahesh further fame in the west. This meditation is a specific kind of mantra meditation that is not taught freely. The only way to learn this mantra technique is to pay someone who is experienced in teaching this technique. However, it is known that, in general the transcendental meditation technique involves usage of mantras that are given to the practitioner based on their gender and age. These mantras are mostly tantric names of Hindu deities. The practitioner is seated with eyes closed in a meditation posture and is required to practice this technique for 15 to 20 minutes twice a day. However, to perform this technique, one has to reach out a professional and be prepared to pay for the privilege.

Yoga Meditations

The term *yoga* means "union." The yoga meditation tradition's roots go back to 1700 B.C. It is the oldest meditation technique on earth and is also one of the most widely known meditation styles in the world. The classic yoga meditation has rules, the asanas or the physical postures, the *pranayama,* or breathing exercises and *pratyahara dharana, dhyana samadhi,* which are the contemplative practices of meditation. Yoga meditation is performed with a goal of reaching spiritual purification and gaining self-knowledge. It is a very rich tradition with various lineages, so there are many techniques involved. One of the most commonly practiced yoga meditations is called "third eye meditation." This technique focuses one's attention on the center point between one's eyebrows, also called the "ajna chakra." The attention on the center of the one's eyes is to silence one's mind and is sometimes accompanied by physically looking with one's eyes shut towards the center point. As hard as it may sound, with practice most practitioners have been able to perform this technique successfully.

Chakra Meditation

The other yoga meditation form is chakra meditation, where the practitioner focuses on the seven chakras of one's body, and these chakras are known as the centers of energy. This is achieved by visualizing and chanting mantras for each chakra. It is most commonly done on the third-eye region chakra, the heart chakra, and the crown chakra or the head chakra.

Gazing Meditation

Gazing meditation is another form of yoga meditation. Here the practitioner is required to fix a gaze on an external object, most typically a candle. This technique is performed with open eyes and then with the eyes closed. This yoga meditation is performed to train concentration and the visualization powers of one's mind. The key point is to keep the image of the candle you saw while your eyes were open even when your eyes have been shut. The object has to be visualized in your mind's eye with your eyes closed. This meditation technique is supposed to be one of the most powerful techniques.

Kundalini Meditation

This is another form of yoga meditation technique. This technique is supposed to be one of the most complex techniques of all. The goal is to awaken the *kundalini* energy at the base of one's spine which helps in developing the various psychic centers in one's body. There are dangers associated with practicing this technique and should be attempted only under the guidance of a qualified yogi. This technique can make you reach enlightenment once you overcome its complexities.

Kriya Yoga

This technique also comes under the yoga meditation umbrella and is suited mostly for people who are seeking spirituality and those who have devotional temperaments. It can be taught by learning self-actualization and realization that is taught widely free of cost around the Internet.

Nada Yoga

Nada Yoga or sound meditation is a technique that focuses on auditory input. It starts with meditating on external sounds where the practitioner focuses on their hearing; this helps to quiet the mind. Then this technique moves forward by focusing the practitioner's hearing senses on the internal sounds of one's mind and body. The goal is to hear the ultimate sound known as *para nada*, which is a sound without vibration "OM."

Pranayama

Pranayama techniques are not meditation per se, but rather, a practice to calm one's mind to prepare the mind for meditation. The most common form of pranayama is the 4444 technique, which literally means to count up to 4 as you breath in, holding your breath for 4 seconds and breathing out for 4 seconds and not breathing for 4 seconds. This requires practitioners to breathe through the nose and not to let the chest move as you let go of the breath through your abdomen region. This breathing technique regularizes mood, and it can be performed anywhere. There are many other yoga meditation techniques, but they are very complex; the ones described above are the most popular techniques practiced around the globe. The simplest one from the ones stated above is the "third eye meditation" that is easy, yet yields great results in a short span. Try practicing this every day for as long as you can.

Obstacles to Meditation

It is normal to expect some obstacles when you begin meditation. Practicing meditation and being mindful is not as easy as we may make it out to be. It will take time to make it a habit and are practicing it regularly. It is common for people to get distracted easily and for their minds to wander. Don't think too much about it when your mind wanders off while you meditate.

As soon as you notice this kind of distraction, just pull your mind back again. It is normal for your mind to be constantly wandering. You may be thinking about your past, worrying about the future, wondering about what you should be doing next. There is always so much to think about and be distracted by. However, while we remain lost in our thoughts, we fail to pay attention to our present. You are probably doing one thing while thinking of another at any given time. This is not a good habit. This is why mindfulness is important. You should not be doing things absentmindedly. You need to learn to focus on the here and now and live in the moment. Mindful meditation helps you to do this.

When you meditate, your mind wanders off to various things. Don't let this hold you back. All you have to do is stop yourself and try to come back to the present instead of thinking of the past or future.

There are three advantages of working with the wandering mind:

You're preparing the brain

Every time you bring your mind back over from its meandering path, you're building the muscle of focus. It really is similar to weightlifting. The mind strays, and you bring it back over and over. Through redundant repetition, you can build mass and increase concentration.

You start to notice thought patterns

When you return into the present moment and notice where you floated off to, you can find components of uncertainty, want, or outrage that you were thinking too much about. This offers greater understanding of problems and challenges. You may also wind up with a mindfulness of stress, trouble, or confusion, which could be a cue that you have to give more consideration to or learn to better manage certain things throughout your life.

You discover that it's not all in your head

You gain a comprehension of the mind-body association and how your thoughts and feelings have a physical manifestation in the body. You start to see how a tight jaw or troubled stomach, for instance, is the manifestation of specific thoughts and feelings in your body.

Five Aspects that Block Meditation

Five key challenges appear as blocks to achieving a meditative state: want, anger, restlessness, drowsiness, and uncertainty. These issues are so common and pervasive in mindfulness meditation practice that numerous books on meditation address how to work around them.

Want or desire

Want, or the desiring mind, is the type of brain that is engrossed with things like needing to feel better. It invests a great deal of energy in dreams, fantasies, and plans. When you feel disgraced, you might be overwhelmed by the craving to become better or extraordinary in some way. It resembles a thirst or craving that rarely eases up.

Anger or outrage

Outrage reflects disapproval of the status quo. You may feel upset at yourself for a perception of being deficient in some way. The angry personality ends up immersed in abhorrence, disdain, or scorn.

Restlessness or fretfulness

Fretfulness resembles a pacing tiger. At the point when your brain is loaded up with fretfulness, it winds up agitated and fumes with uncontrolled energy that is awkward to sit or remain with. It can make you sense that you need to creep out of your skin, similar to when you feel like you have to accomplish something or go elsewhere.

Drowsiness or sleepiness

With drowsiness, your concentration will be dull, and you'll feel slow or tired or have low vitality. Feelings of dishonor, disgrace, or inadequacy may be so overpowering that you feel like you simply need to crumble, vanish, not be here, and rest.

Uncertainty

With uncertainty, you may think about whether meditation fills any need or can help you in any capacity. You may end up loaded up with self-questioning and self-doubt and trust that it is beyond the realm of imagination to ever expect to approve of your identity. This makes it all the easier to fall into the other four obstacles.

Every one of these five obstacles are trying and can impede your training. That is the reason it's so critical to pay attention when they're happening and to have the option to acknowledge and recognize them. As you learned concerning the act of noticing, naming all by itself makes some separation, and this will help loosen the hold of the five obstacles over you. The minute you see you're being weighed down by one of these blocks, you've turned out to be more mindful and can start to venture out of the trap in which you're caught.

Now and then the metaphoric representation of a clear lake is useful in seeing how to go on while facing the obstacles. Every obstruction limits your capacity to plainly observe the beautiful stones at the bottom of the lake. When you're in a state of want, the lake doesn't seem clear; it's shaded with the red color of desire. Your "wants" shade everything. Strive to remain still and inhale mindfulness to quiet your body and psyche.

In case you're irate, the water solidifies and becomes ice, and this also clouds your view. This could possibly be a sign to open up to the light of compassion. With anxiety, the waters are rough. Start to tackle that energy in a useful manner, instead of giving it a chance to kick you in the butt. In case you're sluggish, the waters are filled with green growth. Maybe it's best to wake up and perceive that you aren't going to be here until the end of time. With uncertainty, the lake seems shady or muddy. This is a sign to think about the reason why you're doing this training and what you've found out about yourself up until now. May this give you the motivating force to drive forward.

When you become mindful of the fact that any of the blocks may be present, see how your body and mind feel. Sense the surface of these states and notice what happens when you become engrossed in them. Is it safe to say that you are more at peace by yourself or less?

Chapter Six: Myths About Meditation

You also need to consider the various myths associated with meditation. Busting these myths and understanding the truth about meditation will help you practice it effectively.

Meditation is Just About Concentrating

A lot of people assume that meditation is focused on concentration. However, this is different from what meditation is. Concentrating on something will require a lot of effort and focus. Meditation teaches you how to focus, but in a very relaxing way. It will facilitate better concentration but is not just about this. Meditating will help you achieve a deep state of relaxation, and you will be able to let go of any thoughts or emotions that are crowding your mind.

Meditation is About Religion

Many people believe that meditation originates from and is associated with certain religions. They might be unwilling to practice meditation for this reason alone. However, meditation actually transcends most religions and is not strictly a religious practice. You can meditate regardless of what your religion is. People from any place and background are encouraged to meditate so as to improve their life and sense of well-being.

Meditation Requires You to Sit in the Lotus Posture

If you are not very familiar with meditation, you will usually associate it with the image of someone sitting cross-legged with their eyes closed. However, it is not absolutely necessary to be in this position while meditating. You could actually be walking somewhere and still be meditating. However, it is recommended that you find a comfortable position and sit while meditating to facilitate the practice.

Meditation Involves Hypnosis

For some reason, people also link meditation with hypnosis. However, meditation is the opposite of what hypnotism does to you. When you are hypnotized, you will be unaware of your surroundings and acting subconsciously. When you meditate, it helps to increase your awareness, both internally and externally. So meditation can actually counteract hypnotism.

Meditation Is Only for Old People

No, meditation is not just for the older generation. Meditation can be practiced even if you are a teenager or in your 30s or any other age. It is for everyone and can benefit anyone. Meditation will add value to your life regardless of your age, religion, culture, or gender.

Mediation Requires Hours Every Day

Don't shy away from meditation because you think it will require a lot of time every day. This is not true, and how much time you can dedicate to meditation is entirely up to you. Even 10 minutes a day is enough to experience the positive effects of meditation. However, we recommend that you try to set aside 20 minutes for more improvement.

Meditation Will Make You a Monk

Practicing regular meditation does not make you a monk or any kind of spiritual or religious person. You don't have to give up your current life and become a recluse. You can do it all and still meditate. Meditation will help in enhancing the quality of your life, regardless of what you are doing. It will help you be happier and also help in improving your relations with the people around you.

Meditation Can Only Be Practiced at Certain Times of the Day

There is no limit or restriction on what time of the day you meditate. You can meditate at any time you choose to. You don't have to wake up at 5 a.m. to meditate. There is no such rule. We recommend that you try to meditate at sunrise or sunset. Or try to set a particular time when you can fit meditation into your schedule on a regular basis. Just avoid meditating right after a meal. There is no hard-and-fast rule about when you should meditate. Practicing meditation at the start of your day will help you be more energetic and calm through the rest of the day. Meditating at night will help you let go of your worries of the day and get restful sleep. So no matter when you meditate, it will always work in your favor.

I hope you can now see that these myths are all false and do not apply to the practice of meditation.

Chapter Seven: How to Prepare For Meditation

Meditation does not have any strict rules or restrictions that you have to follow. It can be practiced by anyone, at any place and at any time. However, there are certain things you can do to enhance the experience of meditation and to increase its effectiveness. This chapter is dedicated to helping you prepare for meditation. It is important for each person to find a meditation technique and ways in which they can meditate in the best way for them. For instance, finding the best place or sitting in the right position.

Before we start with the real steps involving meditation, let's talk a bit about the perspective you're embracing when you enter this practice. An indispensable part of any meditation technique is mindfulness. The principal objective here is to develop a familiarity with your body and become more aware of it. You're most likely not accustomed to doing this. So the best step to take is to become increasingly mindful of your body.

As you do this, your body will work to flag any sign of distress it feels with sitting still for any time span. You may find that you experience unfamiliar sensations that may be uncomfortable or even feel pain in spots you could never expect to feel pain in. Many people have complained of the inclination to itch themselves while they are practicing stillness. Don't let this disturb or discourage you, since this is a normal part of the process.

It might be that these sensations were actually present for a long time, yet you were simply too occupied to even think about noticing them. That is why it is important that you pick some comfortable position for practicing meditation, particularly when you are just starting. Simply remember that the little indistinct physical sensations you usually have may be much more amplified amid this period. What's more, from any point of view, it's a good sign. It implies you are building up a more noteworthy sense of mindfulness.

Breathing is the foundation of the experience of meditation. On the off chance that you go to India, you would learn that it is called *prana*. It's firmly identified with life and vitality and for a good reason. Breathing, as you surely understand, is an automatic activity. We do it for twenty-four hours every day, every day of the week without thinking about it at all. Unless you have had an asthma attack, you may not recognize what it's like to wheeze while gasping for air.

At the end of the day, it's an action that you underestimate. Breathing, in a genuine way, is the endowment of life. Through meditation, you increase your familiarity with this automatic activity. You can turn your focus toward this to concentrate on the breathing in, breathing out, rise, and fall of each breath. It progresses toward becoming, fundamentally, the ideal object of mindfulness when you are starting out.

The following tips will help you prepare for meditation:

Find a Place to Meditate

Before you get started with meditation, you need to find a place in which you will not be disturbed. This space should be one where you feel you can relax and focus on meditation. Find a spot in your house or any other place where you can meditate on a regular basis. This is going to be your meditation spot. Keep it clean and neat. Get rid of any distractions. Also, let others know that they should not disturb you when you are there or if they see you meditating. Meditating in random or noisy places can make it hard for you to meditate, especially as a beginner. This space should not be used for doing anything else.

Decide on a Time to Meditate

As discussed before, there is no rule on when you have to meditate. You might be leading an extremely hectic lifestyle. It can seem hard to add something else to your list of things to do. However, meditation will barely take any time, and it will be worth every single minute. The best times to meditate in general are right after you wake up or before you go to bed. Meditating in the morning will help in starting your day the right way. Ending the day with meditation will also help you get relaxed and at peace. However, avoid meditating directly before you sleep. This will make you associate meditation with sleep. However, you may do this if you really want help in sleeping better. Late in the evening around sunset would be ideal if you can't meditate in the morning. So meditate whenever you find time in the day, but avoid meditating after a meal or before a nap.

Get Rid of Disturbances

Your meditation time should be dedicated solely to meditation. Don't let anyone come and disturb you. Turn your phone off. If you meditate at home, let others know that it is your personal time. You can try meditating outside once you are more familiar with meditation. To start with, find a quiet place in your house. Get rid of anything that would normally distract you while meditating.

Set Intentions

Before you meditate, it is a great idea to set an intention. This will allow you to get real value from the time you put in meditating. Your intentions will work as a guiding tool, a north star, for you. Consciously setting intentions before meditation helps in aligning your purpose with the practice. Question yourself about why you are meditating in the first place. It might be for spirituality, for better capacity to concentrate, to improve your relationships, etc. Regardless of what the intention is, you should try to connect with it before meditating.

Practice Poses

You will really be well set up for meditation once you begin performing yoga poses. You get the most advantages when you practice yoga in a more mindful way, so centering your breathing and doing your best to be completely consumed by your training are keys to progress. Your yoga practice will help in relaxing and loosening up your body and to work out any knots that could cause inconvenience during your meditation time. It will likewise help clear out your mind, so you have fewer distracting thoughts drifting around in your brain when it is time to sit and meditate. Furthermore, on the off chance that you require any more inspiration to increase or improve your training, there are many more benefits to yoga and meditation. Rehearsing Hatha yoga or practicing mindfulness meditation for only 25 minutes can actually improve brain capacity and energy levels in a significant way.

Breathing Exercises

Breathing exercises, such as pranayama, help facilitate the

progress from yoga poses to meditation. While your body is retaining the impacts of the asanas, your mind is focusing and getting ready for the task that lies ahead. Centered yogic breathing will allow you to carry your entire self to this new part of your training. Breathing in, holding, and breathing out your breath for a specific number of beats is an incredible method for centering and controlling your breathing. The length of your meditation will decide how much time you spend on breathing activities. However, I like to concentrate on breathing exercises for around 10 minutes before moving into my full meditation practice.

Contentment

Before you start your meditation, it's useful to create as much contentment in your body as could reasonably be expected to have. Since this training is touting the advantages of performing asanas before meditation, that substantial comfort ought to be a need before you go sit on your mat. Do what you can to abstain from showing up excessively hungry or unreasonably full, for instance. Wear open and loose garments. Put your electronic gadgets away or turn them off. You need as few diversions as possible, as these can isolate you from your training. Take a couple of minutes before you start to set a goal for your training. It could be something as straightforward as "remain present" or "facilitate my uneasiness." Whatever your aim is, you can come back to it all through your training to allow yourself to remain on track.

All of these will help you to prepare yourself for meditation on a regular basis.

Chapter Eight: How To Get Started With Meditation

Now that you know more about meditation, you might be itching to get started. So how do you go about meditating? There are a few things you will have to keep in mind. When you first begin meditation, your approach should be as simple as possible. The following pointers will help you go about it the right way.

Don't Expect Too Much

If you didn't think that meditation could help you move mountains, you wouldn't have trouble with it in the first place. Watch those expectations since they might not be realistic.

Meditation is beneficial in light of the fact that - among many other demonstrated advantages for the brain and body - it leads to more overall well-being. In all actuality, however, it requires a specific level of exertion, practice, and dedication to unlock these benefits for your life. A few people experience them very quickly, while others find that it requires an investment of a lot of time and effort.

Assumptions regarding what will happen when you begin to sit on your mat and meditate can be a major impediment to progress. A few people envision that they will encounter extraordinary states of mind, others anticipate a fast track to mental peace, and still others trust that they will develop special powers or abilities as their third eye opens up.

Locate a Tranquil, Agreeable Spot and Sit Upright

If you have set aside a good spot for your meditation practice, that is awesome. In the event that you haven't, any peaceful spot will do.

It's good if you can find a spot to meditate where you are reasonably sure you won't be distracted. It could be your committed meditation corner at home, a quiet space at work or school, outside or some other spot that works for you.

Pick a meditation pose that works best for you. You needn't invest hours sitting in an ideal lotus position; however you should discover a stance and seat that are manageable amid your chosen duration of meditation time. Loosen up your shoulders and get rid of any pressure you feel in your body – particularly in the neck, jaw and other physical strain magnets – however, make sure to keep your back straight. Regardless of whether you are on a chair or a mat, your straight back and good posture will promote mindfulness and prevent the sense of sleepiness that is common for many people when they first begin meditating.

Short and Steady is the Best Approach

Apprentices frequently battle with sitting still for any given period of time. In any case, nobody says that learners should constrain themselves to sitting for ages and ages. Actually, numerous meditation experts recommend that short practice sessions are the most ideal approach for beginners. Regardless, what everybody agrees on is that consistency is most helpful.

Like Lao Tzu stated, "a voyage of a thousand miles starts with the initial step." The initial couple of times you try meditation, try it for two or three minutes at a time. You can sit for longer when it feels right. Some meditators swear by short sessions a few times each day, while others can't cope without their 45-minute morning session.

Your Breath is an Anchor

OK, you're prepared. So now what? Mindfulness, a well-known and open meditation style that has been around for centuries, is usually about sitting in silence and staying in the present. We figure out how to observe our thoughts, sensations, and feelings that show up in the mind stream, and learn to recognize them and let them go. This is meditation: mindfulness, non-judgment, and letting go in the present time and place. We often use our consciousness of the way we breathe as the anchor for our bustling minds and the reason for our meditation practice.

"Thinking" is essentially the way the mind moves. There's no compelling reason to battle with your thoughts—simply give them a chance to come and then release them. Try not to pass judgment on your meditation by the amount of thinking you do or how frequently you have to return to focusing on breathing. Ultimately, you'll find that you can accept whatever emerges in your mind.

Guided Meditations Are of Extraordinary Assistance on this Voyage

Guided meditations remove the mystery from this phase of your mindfulness adventure. The Mindworks App offers guided meditations, Mind Talks by famous meditation specialists, blogs, research studies, and more.

Meditational Chants Play an Important Role

A key part of meditation is using chants or mantras. Mantras are simple words that can profoundly affect your psychological state. Despite the fact that they are basic words, they are amazing in how they can draw a distracted mind back to the center.

There are a couple of mantras that you can use to channel internal harmony, and they include the following:

Om

A standout among the most often utilized chants in the realm of meditation is "Om." It is said to be the most dominant word on the planet as it sends vibrations all over your body when you speak it. Since it is a straightforward mantra, you can recite it as many number of times as you like. Be that as it may, ensure you feel the vibrations traveling through your body as you repeat it.

Aim

Aim represents the female partner of Om and is utilized to channel feminine vitality. By reciting "om" and "aim," you will make a harmony between the male and female viewpoints and have a harmonious existence.

Hrim

Hrim is a groundbreaking chant that is related to creation and protection. One can utilize this chant to increase the sense of self-assurance. It is typically used just after "aim."

Krim

Krim is a word that is used to regulate cortisol levels and leave your psyche with a positive lift. It likewise helps control the adrenaline system and ensures your psyche and body are well adjusted.

Shrim

Shrim is a powerful chant that represents dedication or devotion. This groundbreaking word can be utilized to increase concentration and to put the spotlight on positivity rather than negativity.

Klim

Klim is a chant that finishes the meditation training. Klim is a calming chant that loosens up the psyche and body.

The human body is comprised of 7 concealed chakras that lie in along the centerline of the body. In the event that these chakras are blocked, at that point, you are likely to encounter health problems, both physical and mental in nature. It is recommended to keep these chakras clear to avoid unwanted pressure and nervousness.

There are explicit chants that impact these chakras and help in the clearance of blockages. Let's discuss a few of these:

Lam

Lam helps fix the first chakra. This chakra lies at the base of the spine.

Vam

Vam is utilized to unblock your second chakra, which lies

somewhat over the first chakra.

Ram

The third chakra lies beneath your sternum and can be purged by reciting the word Ram.

Yam

Yam is a chant that can allow you to unblock your fourth chakra. The fourth chakra is also called your heart chakra and controls the remainder of the chakras.

Ham

Ham is a chant used to cleanse the fifth chakra that lies in the focal point of your throat.

Om

As talked about before, Om is a groundbreaking chant that can enable you to purge out your whole chakra framework and promotes overall positive vitality.

Every one of these chants are together called *bija mantras* and as a whole help to keep your chakras cleansed and unblocked.

Ensure that you chant at least one of these words regularly for 20 minutes. Over the long haul once your chakras are altogether cleansed, you will begin feeling light and free of pressure. It will likewise gain control over anger-related issues and will become a better version of yourself.

Chapter Nine: How to Practice Meditation Everyday

Meditation and mindfulness are inseparable. Mindfulness alludes to being available at the present time and guaranteeing that your brain is completely centered on a specific thing.

Here's a look at the association between meditation and mindfulness in detail.

It is said that rehearsing mindfulness is the perfect approach to battling any suffering and a great way of expanding certainty and intelligence. In addition to the fact that it helps increase your own knowledge, it also positively impacts individuals around you.

Mindfulness is regularly shown next to meditation in most Buddhist schools. It enables priests to achieve a more elevated level of inward cognizance.

Mindfulness can be utilized as a way to transport our psyches to a state of quiet. It is utilized to keep diversions under control and increase focus around the present circumstance. The human personality is inclined to diversions and can't concentrate on any one thing at one time. To find a solution to this, mindfulness exercises and tools can be utilized.

It has been said that mindfulness does not move us into the opposite direction; rather, it encourages us to get into a more natural state of being. It teaches us to be available in the present moment and to assimilate to the environment that encompasses us. This reduces pressure and controls anxiety to a large degree.

Mindfulness enables a person to dive deep into their cognizance, and in this manner it aids in upgrading the ability to exercise self-control. The mind will not meander as much and it will be able to focus. A condition of alertness helps in comprehending the environment better and controlling negative responses, for example, rage, loathing, envy, and stress.

By being increasingly present within yourself, you will have the chance to dive deep into your thoughts and draw from the assembled insights that exist inside of you. It can possibly prevent you from buckling under pessimism and avoid experiencing too much stress and nervousness.

You will feel increasingly invigorated and present. Your mind won't get easily occupied and will be able to stay in one spot, where you need your psyche to remain. It has been seen that a great many people try to run from their current situations in anticipation of showing signs of improvement in another situation. Be that as it may, doing this will just exacerbate the issues and make it difficult for them to acknowledge things as they are. It is best to enjoy mindfulness instead, so the circumstance is managed and does not result in unhappiness.

Mindfulness is tied in with giving sharp consideration to the present minute. Focusing on subtleties makes it simpler for an individual to deal with things and be increasingly present in the now. It is imperative to remain positive and present in the moment.

When we become mindful, we don't tend to be angry at little things in our everyday life. Our emphasis is completely on the current moment and what we are doing within that moment. Regardless of whether somebody is trying their hardest to incite anger or to irritate you, you don't get distracted and continue to proceed with your work. On the off chance that you think there should be an adjustment in the setting, at that point it will jump out at you without you having to put in an excessive amount of thought or effort.

How to Approach Rehearsing Mindfulness

As referenced before, mindfulness is tied in with being available in the present moment. You need to assemble your meditations and channel positive energy.

To begin with, here are some mindfulness practices that you can take up on a daily basis:

Mindful counting

A standout among the best and most straightforward mindfulness activities is mindful counting. It involves counting up or down depending on how mindful you wish to be. Begin from 0 and go as far as possible up to 60. When done, go in reverse from 60 as far as possible back down to 0. Proceed with this until your brain is completely present at the time. This procedure can enable you to battle pressure and guarantee that you can analyze the circumstance before making a move.

Mindful breathing

Mindful breathing involves concentrating on your breath. This is like *anulom vilom pranayama* except that you are focused around your normal breathing rather than trying to influence it. Close your eyes and imagine your breath entering your nose and leaving. Take in a deep, full breath that starts from your stomach. You can count to 5 while concentrating on your breath. If you do this for 5 to 10 minutes every day, you will feel totally invigorated, and your mind will feel stimulated. It can also help cut down on distractions and help center around the job that needs to be done.

Mindful eating

Eating is a significantly important part of life. We need to eat to live. Many individuals race through their dinners without pausing to take the time to enjoy it. It is essential to avoid doing this, as it can deplete the nourishment taken in by your body. By enjoying mindful eating, you can bring your psyche once again to the center and make the most of your suppers. It is normal to go through at least 30 minutes for every dinner. Close your eyes while biting what you eat. Focus on the flavors, ensuring you appreciate each part of the meal. Do this for each of the times you eat your main meals.

Mindful exercise

Exercise is a fundamental part of life if you want to be healthy. If you don't work out at all and are entirely sedentary, your body begins discharging more cortisol as a reaction to stress. In any case, through exercise you can increase the secretion of serotonin in your body. It is ideal to practice mindfulness while working out. Begin by rising early and doing stretches for your whole body. Take a walk or go running. Keep your focus on the action and the environment. In the event that you have a pet, try to walk him/her regularly. Try not to hurry through the process and try to appreciate each part of it.

Mindful music

Music is among the most common stress busters on the planet. By mindfully tuning in to music, you can get rid of your pressure and nervousness. Tune in to mindful music and try focusing on the different beats and melodies. In case you don't have time schedule-wise to just sit down and listen to music, put your earphones on while doing household tasks and reel in the harmony.

Mindful showering

Most people tend to neglect to value the small details of everyday life and always seem in a rush to complete some assignment or another. One incredible pressure buster is a long shower. A nice long shower can seemingly wash away the fatigue of your day. A shower cleans your body and also quiets your mind down. Try taking 30 minutes in the shower entertaining yourself and remain completely centered around the action. Begin by turning on the shower and picture yourself being under a stream or waterfall. Get the bar of cleanser and smell it to stir up your senses. Roll the bar over your body and focus on the trail it goes along. Foam up and take as much time as necessary in washing it away. This experience can help you get over an unpleasant day.

Mindful cooking/tasks

It is critical to be mindful while preparing meals and performing your usual errands. Try not to sit in front of the TV or have any other distractions. You ought to be completely centered on the job that needs to be done.

Mindful dreams

Your dreams can tell you a great deal about your subliminal personality. Truth be told, they hold the key to why you may experience pressure and uneasiness. So as to understand them better, it is ideal to take part in mindfulness envisioning.

Repeat the expression "I will recall my dream" 10 or more times before going to bed. It will allow you to recollect your dreams better in the first part of the day. Keep a book and pen to record these dreams when you wake up. Attempt to find an example in your dream with the aim to show signs of improvement. When you discover what is upsetting you, you can take a shot at tackling the issue through meditation.

Let's discuss meditation for specific intents and how to go about it.

Meditation for Losing Weight

We all, in general, tend to go to food at any point that we are worried about something in everyday life. At the point when problems overpower us, the vast majority of us will, in general, eat our stress, and afterward, we experience a cycle of self-blame and regret the choice we made. In time, this cycle can affect how we feel about ourselves.

With guided meditation, you will recollect how to feel better and will also be able to better comprehend your relationship with food. During times of stress, you will find out about relinquishing this type of tension, and to experience all that is right and natural.

The experience of following this guided meditation will be amplified if you find yourself an agreeable and comfortable spot.

Try to make sure that there is no distraction from anything or anybody for thirty minutes.

You have to pick a position where you can lie down or possibly just sit comfortably for the duration of this activity. It would be wise to turn off your phone or put it on silent mode. Your calls and texts can wait.

At this point, you have to close your eyes and prepare yourself for a profound feeling of unwinding and a greater sense of well-being. Keep in mind that this is your personal time and take hold of the chance to escape from the stress of the world you live in. You would now be able to give up all unwanted habits and figure out how to support your inner soul.

At this specific moment, there is nothing that you have to stress over. You find a sense of contentment, and you are sheltered. You will allow the troubles of the day to dissipate so you can face your own internal identity. With your eyes closed, inhale deeply and gradually through your nose and then breathe out through your mouth. When you take in a breath, you are taking all that is great and positive about this world into your body, and when you exhale, you are relinquishing all pressures and superfluous anxieties.

Now you have to breathe in once more. Take in a breath gradually through your nose as you count to four.

One, two, three, and four.

With your lungs now full of oxygen, hold your breath for two seconds.

One and two.

Now you can breathe out gradually through your mouth. You have to breathe out as you count to four.

One, two, three, and four.

When you take in a breath, you can gradually feel your stomach grow when you feel the air enter your lungs. Inhale until you have a feeling that your lungs are completely filled with air.

Try to control the exhalation of air and ensure that you inhale out entirely.

You have to proceed with this cycle of breathing rhythmically.

Breathe into the count of four.

Hold your breath for a count of two.

Let out your breath to the count of four.

You can resume breathing as you ordinarily do, and you will feel all the strain in your body gradually disperse.

Recognize that your body is currently beginning to feel progressively more relaxed. Your arms and legs will begin to feel heavier.

Loosen up the pressure in your lower back, center back and upper back. Usually, we tend to store a lot of tension in our shoulders. Find a way to discharge it. When you let go of the pressure you feel in your body, you can feel your body unwind.

Extend your neck so that there is space between your ears and shoulders. When you gradually extend your neck, you can feel the cushion you are lying on or the seat that you are perched on supporting your back.

Examine your body and check to see if there are any regions of stress left. On the off chance that you feel that there are a few, at that point, you have to purposely tighten the muscles there and let go. When you do this, you can feel your body relax. You will feel it as the tension is leaving your body.

At this point, you have to enter into a state of profound meditation.

To do this, you have to proceed with regular breathing.

Envision that you are currently in an amazingly beautiful garden with delicate beams of daylight falling on you.

You can see an arched gate that is cut into a rising cliff.

Your environment looks very serene, and you start to feel better.

You can see beautiful sandy shorelines behind you and light blue skies above you.

Now you are gradually advancing toward the arched entryway. The entryway is right within your reach; the wood feels warm under your fingers. As you trail your fingers over the entryway, you can feel a sense of energy and marvel as you envision what lies beyond the gate.

To enter, you have to keep your mind open to the miracles that lie ahead. Put your hand on it and gradually turn the handle.

As you enter, you can see a lavish and splendid green rainforest.

The air feels under the canopy, and is a much-needed change from the sun-soaked shoreline a couple of minutes back.

Take a full breath in and then breathe out to take hold of this feeling of harmony.

As you stroll forward, you see a trail that leads through this beautiful rainforest.

As you look into it, you can see the parts of an azure sky that is spotted with delicate, cotton-like clouds.

Keep examining the sky surrounding you.

You are encompassed by tall, mahogany trees that reach up towards that sky.

You wonder about the darker bark of the trees that appears to have a delicate, sweet scent.

Space is constrained here; however, you are appreciative of the trail that leads you through this spot of miraculous nature.

You can tune in to the pleasant chirping of the birds surrounding you.

It feels like the woodlands have woken up around you.

This appeals to you in every way, and you get to experience nature in its perfect form.

Consider what would happen if you stripped back your own life and were to live more in tune with nature. How much better would you feel?

Just a little bit of daylight can infiltrate onto the forest floor. In this way, you move farther in the wild, and you can see the flashes of extraordinary blue butterflies moving around you.

You can hear the running water that is flowing in the distance with a melodic sound, and you feel compelled to move in the direction the sound is coming from.

As you take in the miracle of the amazing nature surrounding you, you move towards the bigger territory of the woodlands that in turn will guide you towards a small stream of water.

There are stepping stones here that lead you to a pool of water that is completely clear. You can see right through the crystal clear water. The pool of water is encompassed by green plants.

You walk nearer to the pool, and you notice plants with beautiful berries all around.

There are a few plants bearing fruits, and everything looks rich, lush, and enticing.

You take a nibble of these berries, and you can feel a burst of flavors.

The berries taste good, and you can feel this flavor as it clears a path down to your stomach.

Your body feels invigorated.

There are stones that are all around and over the water, and as you walk, you feel at one with nature.

You see cut out steps higher in the stones, and you begin to climb up them.

It is a very easy climb, and it feels practically effortless.

You feel a great stretching sensation in your muscles when you hold the stones for grip.

There is no fear of falling.

As you grasp the stones and advance up, you feel less weighted down, more grounded, and your body feels toned.

You feel precisely how you need to feel and how you need to be.

You pull yourself up ever higher. You are gradually advancing towards the shelter.

You can feel it as the air becomes cleaner.

You begin to take in the pure oxygen and let go of any stress you are clutching onto.

Your usual problems appear as though they are miles away.

You think about how great you feel right now.

You keep on advancing towards the shade.

You don't need to fear the height since it is sheltered, and you can't fall.

You don't feel worn out or depleted of energy. In this world, you feel fit, sound, and experience a bounty of vitality. You are resolved to get to the top and see the view from the highest point.

Envision going up every one of these steps until you reach the last step and the apex of your adventure.

You are now at a huge platform, and from there you can see the top of the trees.

Right opposite you, there is a stone face with water falling down it. The water is foaming up on its way down the stones, and the sight of the waterfall is entrancing.

You can reach up and touch the mists. You can feel the mist surround you.

The unending sky looks amazing.

Picture all these brilliant impressions that course through your body.

You experience a feeling of unwinding. Every last bit of your being feels better and more relaxed.

Take this moment and picture yourself stretching.

Reach up high and feel the sensation as you lengthen your spine. Now, keep your back level and move in front and down. Allow your body to unwind forward. Revel in the great stretch you can feel in the backs of your legs-there is no torment, only joy. Your spine begins to relax; from your lower back up to your neck as you lift your arms. Your neck and your head unwind as you lie on the large platform.

Keep your arms behind your head. Draw in your center muscles and attempt to lift your shoulder and your head up towards the mist up above.

Imagine yourself lifting and connecting with those core muscles while you pull in your stomach and tighten your belly. The majority of these actions will make you feel so great.

Now begin to unwind a little.

Start focusing on how you breathe. Breathe in as you spread your chest and breathe out gradually.

It is time that you begin to like the individual you are. The time has come to feel confident and content and find inner harmony. Here in this rainforest, you are allowed to explore and be the individual that you have always wanted to be.

Relinquish any undesirable dietary patterns. The time has come to be thoughtful toward your body and to support and secure your body. Unhealthy food will prevent you from doing this.

Always repeat all the affirmations taught here to yourself and have confidence in each word.

Put stock in the message and the power of these words to completely change you.

I will change my impression of my body.

I increase my sense of self-esteem.

I will change my dietary patterns with the goal of seeing my food as fuel and nutrition as opposed to a source of comfort and stress relief.

I will trade binging on food for breathing exercises and guided meditation.

I will begin exercising and changing the way I look and feel.

I will make a journal and plan how to work out.

I am prepared to confront my inner feelings of fear and make the necessary positive changes.

Sit in silence for a minute and absorb these affirmations within you.

The time has come to feel positive about your life.

The time has come to confront any weight issues head-on.

You have the ability to do this.

You can always come back to this rainforest and experience the marvels of nature. You can find your internal strength and motivation in this place of refuge.

You are focused, and you hold peace and harmony within you.

Appreciate every minute and the harmonious feelings that you experience.

Take in a breath and then let it out.

Hold onto your feeling of harmony and your longing to sustain your body in a healthy way.

Take in another breath and let it out.

You will change your relationship with food.

Take in a breath and let it out.

Gradually open your eyes as you count to three.

One, two, and three.

Now, you are back in the present.

Slowly stretch your body and keep on taking full breaths.

Acknowledge how great you feel at this time.

Keep in mind your intention to improve your wellness and overall well-being.

Come back to this place of refuge of yours at whatever point you need to in order to improve your well-being.

You can utilize this method whenever you feel strained or anxious.

Meditation to Control Anger

Locate a peaceful spot and close your eyes. Count to 10. Consider counting backward so your mind invests additional effort and it works to distract you.

Sit in a quiet spot and close your eyes. Pull in 10 to 15 full breaths and focus on the oxygen that is entering and the exhalation that is leaving your body.

In the event that you are in an open natural space, move towards a component of nature, for example, trees, ocean, or grass. Remain by it and take in full breaths.

In the event that a specific individual is angering you, go to a peaceful place and close your eyes. Concentrate on the individual's positive characteristics and battle the negative emotions. This applies to different circumstances too. Make sure you concentrate more on the positive aspects of the current circumstance.

Even with your bustling work routine, take time to make a rundown of things that are troubling you. Sit in the lotus posture and practice breathing exercises. Think of each issue consciously and pull them into your conscious mind and breathe it out of your body.

Keep a diary to write down about any such anger inducing scenes. Recognizing what your triggers are can enable you to be more proactive and be more meditative as you assume a position to battle your anger.

Meditation for Promoting Physical Healing

Locate a comfortable spot for yourself and sit in a casual position.

Allow your body to unwind.

Take in a breath through your nose and inhale it out through your nose.

Take slow and long breaths.

Take a breath in for cleansing and discharge all the unwanted pressure or stress in your body as you exhale out.

You can begin to feel the relaxation begin at the base of your feet. It feels like you are entering into a bath filled up with warm water. You will feel calm and loose. Give in to this process of relaxation, and allow it to spread from your toes to your lower legs, upward towards your knees and then the upper legs.

Give this chance to your body to allow it to unwind and let it spread all through your body.

Feel the relaxation spread to your hips, pelvic region, stomach, lower back, chest, and your upper back. Give this relaxation a chance to spread to your upper arms, elbows, wrists, hands, palms, fingers, and the fingertips. At that point, let it spread to your collarbones, shoulders, neck, and your head.

Give your whole body a chance to unwind, one section at any given moment.

Presently, your whole body is calm and loose from your head to your toes.

Take in a breath, hold your breath and after that inhale out. By doing this, every muscle in your body will unwind gradually. Allow the breath to flow out through your nose delicately.

When you discharge the breath, you let go of any tension that was remaining in your body. Keep on taking in breaths easily and gradually. You have to check your body for any other regions of remaining pressure. In the event that you sense any strain in a specific spot, you have to guide your ability to achieve relaxation into that region and let it oust any tension that remains.

Picture that the air that you are taking in will purify your body and it will expel any unnecessary stress. Envision that each breath you take allows a sense of relaxation to flow into your body.

Now begin to picture that at whatever point you breathe out, you are breathing out any pressure present in your body.

Now it is time to unwind and appreciate this sense of calmness you feel.

Concentrate on your body and consider all the recuperating that it needs.

Invoke a picture in your psyche of your current situation. Imagine all the hazards you face, all the health conditions you may be experiencing, either physical or mental. Whatever it is, you have to mend it. You have to envision this issue in your psyche.

Concentrate on the particular area of trouble.

Picture this hazardous region under dark shade and think about the relaxing healing as a burst of light. Imagine that this relaxation light is continually coursing through your body. You have to visualize that this light is moving towards the dark territory that is problematic.

Your body is equipped for recuperating itself. The healing relaxation advances your immune system, strengthens, and promotes the development of healthy tissues, expels toxic components from your body, and helps in cleansing your body.

The healing light of relaxation is delicately flowing through your body. It is gradually flowing and contacting the edges of this dark territory.

You can see that the recuperating light carries little bits of the dark zone with it. You can see that your body is diverting these particles of darkness out of your body as you exhale out.

You have to take a full breath in.

You are breathing in well-being, calm, and the capacity to recuperate.

Now let go of your breath.

You are breathing out any pressures, issues, and feelings of illness from your body.

Give this healing light of relaxation a chance to keep on moving around the dark region. You can bit by bit observe that the dark zone is contracting.

Soon, the dark territory is going to be totally wrapped in this healing light of relaxation.

You can see that this territory is getting to be lighter and all that is unwanted is being completely removed from your body.

Envision that your innate immunity is making an effort to aid you in recuperation. Visualize every one of the cells that your body needs to recuperate. Envision how every one of these cells is working to help in healing your body.

Envision the healing light of relaxation moving through your body.

Picture your whole body becoming completely relaxed.

The dark territory is lighter in shade than it was before, and it is getting lighter every second.

All the agony and inconvenience it caused to you is being diverted from your body.

Your body is recuperating itself.

Take a full breath in to purge yourself. Exhale out anything that your body does not need or want.

Unwind for two or three minutes and envision the healing process that is going on inside your body.

Have faith in your body's capacity to mend itself.

This makes you feel relaxed and calm.

Now is the time for you to wake up and come back to your reality.

On the count of three, it is time to awaken and arise.

One, two, and three.

Meditation for Body Image Relaxation

Get yourself a good spot for sitting comfortably.

Ensure that you are wearing loose clothing, and nothing feels too tight.

Take in a breath gradually, hold your breath, and exhale out.

With your breath, take in all the inspiration you need and exhale out all the pessimism from your body.

When you do this, you can begin to feel the pressure moving out of your body.

Begin to examine your body rationally and see whether there is any tension in your body.

Begin with the tips of your toes to the highest point of your head.

You can feel positive vitality coursing through your body and purifying everything along the way.

If you still feel any areas of stress in your body, focus around those regions as you take a full breath in. You are taking in relaxation, and you are relinquishing all of the stress.

Let's review a few self-perception affirmations, and you can use these at any time you need to.

Every affirmation is completely valid, regardless of whether or not it seems to be at the present time.

Take a chance to begin the affirmations at this time.

I am all right the way I am.

I acknowledge myself however I am.

I accept my body regardless of how it looks.

I am a decent person.

I am perfect just as I am.

I don't need to think of another person's concept of perfection in order to feel good about myself.

I am immaculate, even with every one of my flaws. They make me interesting.

I acknowledge myself.

I don't pass judgment on myself.

I cherish myself.

Now since you have repeated these affirmations, see how you feel.

How was it to say these or tune in to these sentences?

It is all right to feel whatever you are feeling, positive or negative.

Acknowledge every one of the emotions that you experience.

Pause for a minute to just unwind.

Take a full breath in, and as you exhale out, let go of every single pointless stressor you were clutching on to.

Now it's time to come back to your reality.

Count down from five to one, and then awaken. You will feel revived and prepared to come back to your day-by-day life.

Five, four, three, two, and one.

I hope these meditation practices help you overcome some common issues in your everyday life. Meditation can be directed towards any concern you have to help you improve your well-being and just lead a happier life overall.

Chapter Ten: Suggestions/Tips for Meditation

Now that you have come to the end of this book, we will share some more suggestions and tips to allow you to continue with your meditation practice. These are not aimed at making you an expert but just to assist you on the journey. It is not necessary to try all of these tips at the same time. You can try one or two at a time to see if they help you. There will be some that work better than others. Find what's right for you.

Begin Your Practice with 2-Minute Sessions

It may sound like it's pointless to meditate for just two minutes but trust us when we say it's anything but. It's simple to do this and is the easiest way for a beginner to learn to practice meditation. Just dedicate two minutes of each day to meditation. Continue this for a week. It's easier to follow through with these two minutes than pressuring yourself to sit still for half an hour. Once you get used to these two minutes, you can add more minutes the next week and so on. You will soon see that you easily meditate at least 15 minutes daily after a couple of weeks, and that will be more than enough time for most. So don't worry and don't make excuses about not having time. Everyone has two minutes to meditate.

Practice Your Meditation Every Morning

A lot of people say that they will meditate every day in the beginning, but most of them fail to follow through with this claim. Don't assume that you will always remember or be inclined to do it. Commit yourself to meditating every single morning after you wake up. After you wash up, just set aside a few minutes for this and you will see how much better your day goes. Early mornings are considered the best time to meditate.

Don't Worry About the Process and Focus on Beginning the Practice

When people start meditating or think about starting it, they often waste a lot of time and energy on worrying about how they should go about it. They waste time in looking up too many methods, finding the perfect mat to sit on, learning chants, etc. All of these are a part of the practice but not the *essence* of it. You need not spend so much time on this and should try to go with the flow. Just find a comfortable place to sit where you won't be disturbed or distracted by anything. Sitting right on the ground is completely fine and so is sitting on a chair. To begin with, focus less on all this and more on spending two whole minutes just meditating. The stress of these trivial things will hinder your meditation. So try to get more used to meditating itself and worry about all this later.

Pay Attention to How You Feel

Once you begin meditating, you need to try being more attuned to your personal feelings. Pay attention to how you feel and how this practice is affecting your body. Tune in to the thoughts that pass through your mind. Don't focus on them but notice them as they flow past. Be accepting of all the feelings and thoughts that you experience during meditation. Nothing is wrong or right; so don't judge yourself for any of it.

Count as You Breathe

Breathing is an important aspect of meditation. Find the right place to meditate and then close your eyes as you sit comfortably. Start concentrating solely on your breathing. Focus on your breath as you inhale and exhale. Notice how you take in air through your nose and into your lungs. Pay attention as it leaves your body. When you take in a breath, count one. Count two when you breathe out. Continue the counting as you keep breathing and focus on this alone. It will help you focus more.

It Is Okay for Your Thoughts to Wander

The human mind tends to wander a lot, and you need to be more accepting of it as you meditate. You don't have to assume that you are not allowed to think anything when you meditate. This can be impossible to avoid, at least at first. When you meditate, try not to think but be accepting when thoughts come in. When you notice your concentrating wandering off from your meditation to your thoughts, push back your mind slowly. It can be disappointing, and you might feel like you are doing it wrong, but it is all right. Just slowly come back when your mind wanders away.

Be More Accepting

Like we already said, it is natural for thoughts to appear as you meditate. Don't be defensive and try to push them away all the time. Instead, be more accepting and allow them to come and pass. Take note of these thoughts, and you can focus on them later. But as you meditate, allow them to come and go naturally. Your thoughts are a part of you, and you need to accept and forgive yourself for everything that you are.

Don't Stress About the Method of Meditation

You might be worried that you are meditating the wrong way at first. A lot of people get stressed about this and think it will be ineffective if they don't practice the right method or do it the right way. The truth is, there is no perfect method of meditation. You can try the various methods we have mentioned and use them as guidelines, but ultimately, you need to do what feels best for you.

Your Mind Doesn't Have to be Empty While Meditating

Some people think that meditation means getting rid of all thoughts and clearing the mind completely. However, this is not true and can be almost impossible for most people. It can be possible to clear your mind out sometimes, but for the most part, it's not what is essential for meditation. It's normal to have thoughts, and you don't have to force yourself to push them all out. Just be more accepting of them and let them pass without focusing on them. Work more on your concentration, and you will see that it gets easier to reduce distracting thoughts over time.

Take Some Time to Accept Your Thoughts and Feelings

As we mentioned repeatedly, having thoughts while meditating is totally normal. When a thought passes through your mind, it is okay to take a moment and pay attention to it. In the beginning, we recommend to just let the thoughts pass and focus more on breathing. But over time, you can try noticing more of your thoughts too. You should avoid focusing on anything negative and try to bring in more positive thoughts. When you notice your thoughts, you will be able to learn more about yourself. But only allow yourself a moment for this before continuing with your meditation.

Learn a Little More about Yourself Every Day

Meditation is not just about improving your focus or being better able to concentrate. It is about helping your mind develop too. When you become more accepting of your thoughts and feelings, you will learn a lot about yourself. Don't push yourself too hard to think or feel a certain way. Be accepting and learn about yourself. No one can know you better than yourself.

Be Your Own Friend

You need to try learning more about yourself, but this should not be done with a mindset of self-analysis and judgment. Instead, be kinder to yourself. Think of it like learning more about someone you *like*. Accept who you are and be your friend. Don't be cruel and judgmental towards yourself.

Pay Attention to Your Body

After you get better at counting breaths and meditating, you can try something else. Now you should try focusing on your body. Do this with one body part at a time. As you meditate, focus on a specific body part and try to pay attention to how it feels. Start with the lowest point in your body and move on until every part of your body has been acknowledged. This will allow you to pay attention to your body and learn more about it. You will be able to notice if something feels wrong too.

Be Truly Determined

You cannot say you will meditate regularly and then fail to follow through. It is important to dedicate yourself to this practice. Don't take it lightly. Make sure you stick to this resolution for at least a few weeks. Motivate yourself to follow through with it every day. It will soon become a habit, but not if you lack determination right from the beginning.

Meditate, Regardless of Where You Are

It doesn't matter if you're on a trip or have to work overtime on some days. Don't skip your meditation practice. You might reduce the amount of time you can dedicate to it, but you should still meditate. You don't necessarily need that meditation corner in your home for this. It can be done while sitting in a car or even while you sit in your office chair.

Use Guided Meditations

It may seem hard to meditate when you first begin. Guided meditations can be instrumental in this case. Use these audio or video files to help you get started. They are very simple and accommodating regardless of whether you are a beginner or have practiced for some time.

Have Someone to Be Accountable To

If you keep your resolution to meditate to yourself, you are less likely to follow through with it. It will be easy to give up because there is no one to berate you over it. This is why you need to have someone that will hold you accountable. It could be a friend or family member. Just keep checking in with them, and they will help you stay on track. You can also find someone to practice it regularly. This could be someone you live with, work with, or even someone who will go to lessons with you. Finding a network of people who are interested in meditation will help in reinforcing your new good habit. These people can help support you through your journey. You can find online forums or communities of people who practice meditation too.

Conclusion

As you come to the end of this book, I would first like to thank you for investing your time. I hope you found it resourceful. The aim of the book was to introduce you to the amazing possibilities that come with the practice of meditation. Adding meditation to your daily routine will benefit you in so many ways. It is not a choice you will ever regret. You can try any of the various methods mentioned in this book and you will get only positive results.

Meditation will help you become more disciplined and focused in everything you do. It will help you relax and take a break from all your troubles. It will help you to improve your physical, mental, and spiritual health over time. You will be able to live a happier life and let go of the things that previously stressed you out on a daily basis. The best part is that you will only have to give 10-15 minutes of your day just to reap all these rewards. So find a quiet place and take the time to practice meditation from today forward. You will notice positive changes if you start sooner rather than later.

If you found this book helpful, please recommend it to your friends and family and consider leaving a positive review. Meditation is a great practice for everyone.

Thank you for reading, and I wish you the best.

References

Gyalwa, T. (2019). Top 10 Easy Tips on How to Meditate by Trungram Gyalwa, PhD | Mindworks. Retrieved from https://mindworks.org/blog/top-tips-on-how-to-meditate/

Cosley, R. (2019). How to Meditate - Meditation Techniques by Paramhansa Yogananda. Retrieved from https://www.ananda.org/meditation/how-to-meditate/

Cosmillo, L. (2019). 6 Simple Meditation Techniques For "Real People." Retrieved from https://www.mindbodygreen.com/0-16452/6-simple-meditation-techniques-for-real-people.html

Buddhist Meditation Techniques & Practices (2019). Retrieved from https://mindworks.org/blog/buddhist-meditation-techniques-practices/

How To Prepare For Meditation. (2019). Retrieved from https://blog.sivanaspirit.com/md-sc-how-to-prepare-for-meditation/

Stahl, B., & Flowers, S. (2016). Overcome These Five Common Obstacles to Meditation - Mindful. Retrieved from https://www.mindful.org/overcome-these-five-common-obstacles-to-meditation/

Where Does Meditation Come From? Meditation History & Origins. (2019). Retrieved from https://mindworks.org/blog/history-origins-of-meditation/

How to Start Meditating: 5 Meditation Techniques for Beginners. (2019). Retrieved from https://mindworks.org/blog/how-to-start-meditating/

Meditation for Beginners: 20 Practical Tips for Understanding the Mind : zen habits. (2016). Retrieved from https://zenhabits.net/meditation-guide/

Made in the USA
Monee, IL
06 March 2020